AMERICANS

CAN live Happily Ever After-2 after Covid 19

Helping you, your children, family, block and city, county and state to live happily ever after Covid 19

ELIZABETH WILEY MA JD, POMO ELDER

Order this book online at www.trafford.com
or email orders@trafford.com

Most Trafford titles are also available at major online book retailers.

 www.trafford.com

North America & international
toll-free: 844 688 6899 (USA & Canada)
fax: 812 355 4082

Our mission is to efficiently provide the world's finest, most comprehensive book publishing service, enabling every author to experience success. To find out how to publish your book, your way, and have it available worldwide, visit us online at www.trafford.com

ISBN: 978-1-6987-0998-7 (sc)

ISBN: 978-1-6987-0997-0 (e)

Print information available on the last page.

Trafford rev. 11/20/2021

CONTENTS

INTRODUCTION:

Our books are written as on ongoing series for high risk youth, veterans, and first responders as well as their parents and those who are raising them.

One of the reasons for starting this series was we, as special needs teachers, as therapists, as Directors of programs and private schools for high risk youth began to recognize how many of the children and youth were children of veterans, grandchildren of veterans, and also first responders.

We then noticed the numbers of minority children and poverty level financial back grounds were the reality for high risk children and youth. We saw children of Mothers who had been as young as NINE at the birth of their child among the high risk students. Whether rich, or poverty level, we saw children of alcohol, sexual, and drug addictions.

We saw children as young as 18 months labeled with an alphabet of mental health disorders, medicated and put into "special schools" where in fact media found they were often warehoused, abused, and not taught at all. Upon seeing a news story about the schools discovered at some of the licensed sites, in which children and teens often did not have desks, or chairs to sit on, let alone proper educational supplies and equipment for special learning program, we joined with others, and designed programs.

We were naive enough to think our work, offered FREE in most cases, would be welcomed especially as we offer it free and often through research projects, but, it was NOT valued or wanted.

What? we asked?

We went back to college and while earning degrees we had apparently NOT needed while working with children of the very rich in expensive private schools, we did research projects to document our findings. To find ways to overcome the problems. Again, our work was NOT valued or wanted.

One of our associates, who had asked many of us to volunteer in a once a month FREE reading program in the local public schools, was held back for almost two years doing paperwork and proving her volunteers, most of them parents of successful children, teens and adults, could read a first five years book and teach parents how to read those books to their own children. She was a Deputy United States Prosecutor, and had recruited friends from all levels of law enforcement, child and family services, education and volunteer groups that served children and families.

None the less, we continued our work, met a fabulous and expensive Psychiatrist who was building his own server system and the first online education project after creating a massive and encompassing medical examination study guide for graduate medical students to assist them in passing global and national medical examinations for licensing.

We worked with a team of citizens and specialists in education who had created a 39 manual project for students, parents and teachers to be able to learn on their own.

This series of books includes ideas, history and thoughts from the students, the parents, and professionals who work with these situations.

Jesus was told, don't have children wasting your time, and he responded, let the children come.

Our work is to bring children to us, and to those who have the heart and love to develop the uniqueness and individuality of each of God's creations. Many of them are of different religions, and beliefs, and many are atheists but believe fully in the wonder and uniqueness of every human.

To all who have helped and continue to help children and anyone wanting to learn, we thank God and we thank you.

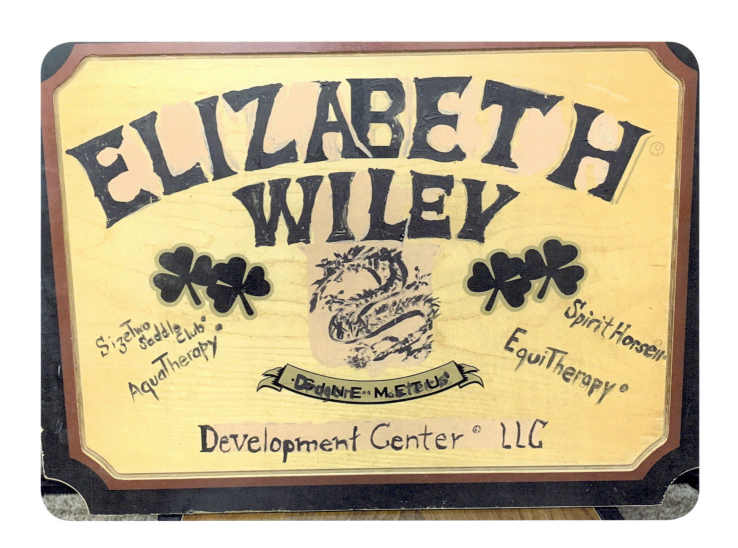

Tee shirts we designed for 5 year global spay and neuter million more spay project for OUR Community ROOTS AND SHOOTS PROJECT (you can start your own local environmental.jpgTee shirts we designed for 5 year global spay and neuter million more spay project for OUR Community ROOTS AND SHOOTS PROJECT (you can start your own local environmental

CHAPTER ONE

America CAN live happily ever after: after Covid

A year out of our lives, not just as an individual, a city, county, state, or nation, the entire world was brought down by the virus known as Covid-19. HOW can we unify and work together, as a family, a block, a school, a city, a county, a state, a nation and a global family of different nations.

List all you personally know who died, or were severely ill, lost their homes, their jobs, their family members to Covid-19.

Write how these losses made you feel, are you learning to heal, and to help others to heal. There are many groups forming locally to all to help each one heal. Join one as fits you if needed.

CHAPTER TWO

Personal Loss And Healing

Healing is helped by finding others and talking to others. Finding groups that help us all heal together.

There is a joke that says, those who made it through either made it being drunk, chunk(over-eating and gaining weight) or hunk(those who realized they had to survive and began to take action to physically, emotionally and spiritually improve themselves for the NOW and for when things go back to "normal".

Are you a hunk?

A chunk

A drunk(this includes both prescription and none-prescription drugs and medications.

What are YOU personally going to do, or are already starting to do to heal, and find a new way of life after Covid?

CHAPTER THREE

Family (or close friends) and close friends

Love one another........The Bible

John 15-17

Most religions ask us to love one another. When asked what are the important commandments, Jesus through John told us Honor God, body, mind and soul, and then to love one another AS, not better than, not less than ourselves.

This creates three responsibilities for each of us. No matter what our religion, or no religion, we are asked to HONOR our Creator, to let our life be a light to shine on to all, to glorify our Creator.

Second: To love ourselves, if we do not love ourselves, we can NOT love anyone else.

Third: to love one another.

What an amazing world we would have if every single person somehow, miraculously decided in one second to follow these three ways of living.

List ways you can love yourself?

List ways you can love one another:

One of the best ways to love others is to simply stop thinking we know how to "save" them and just love them, as they are. Yet this does NOT mean we have to put up with bad behavior of those we love and interact with on a regular basis. This may mean we need to have a serious talk with some family members and friends and let them know we NEED to figure out how we can work out our relationship while they are doing things that make OUR life scary, dangerous, or demeaned.

This is NOT about a judgmental discussion of THEIR faults, it is about our love for them, but how can they help US to be around them without their behavior putting us at risk, or our children and families at risk.

Many family see other family members ONLY in public and at well attended family gatherings where everyone is able to keep the person company so they do NOT steal. People keep their purses, wallets, and phones in their vehicle trunks, the keys in their pockets. It is hard to bring these changes about, but it often helps the person to realize their behavior is harming others they love, and who love them.

MENTAL illness (this includes addictions, which includes relationship addictions to abusive persons). One of the saddest and most painful parts of any family is a person who has some form of mental illness. PTSD for veterans and many first responders, such as critical hospital staff, nurses and doctors, and fire fighters, mental health professionals, and police is NOT considered a mental illness, it is a horrible result of living through trauma that most of us could not live through. BUT PTSD harms other family members, and anyone who cares for the person. This is NOT about blame, it is about working with professionals to help the person want to get the help they need. Often victims of PTSD are dangerous to themselves and to their family members. GET PROFESSIONAL help yourself to help YOU deal safely with those suffering PTSD. There are veteran groups, one is named Vet Hunters, they train other veterans to go out and find PTSD veterans and get them to the help they need. These groups usually need community support. We have found many groups that take the grants, and the public accolade of helping veterans, but when Vet Hunters, or other first line helpers bring in veterans to get help, they are turned away, or treated unprofessionally making their problems worse.

List members of your family (even yourself) who needs help to recover balance in their life, or find balance and support to not be a danger to themselves or others. Addicts are NOT trendy non-conforming people, they are people who daily put their own lives at risk, steal both love and money (or things to sell) from family, friends, and anyone else they can steal from. This "might" include you......create this list from an idea of helping live with love for that person, but not be at risk, this includes yourself.

For each of the persons you listed, make a list of things you can do to show love, and to communicate the need for change to be safe and feel loved yourself.

CHAPTER FOUR

Your block, your city

Show love, and expect love in your block, your city, your schools, your public buildings and projects, and community political elected persons.

America, the America so many people want to come to, USED to be commits oriented. Today that is no longer true. Even families are broken apart by the hate, and division spewed by politicians over the past few decades.

In the sixties, no matter millions of peaceful walks, music in the park BE INs or representative events (I do not like the word protest, and never do anything anti-) people might have argued about policy, but after an election the country came back as one, to attempt to resolve the issues raised before, during and by the election. It was about policy, not political games. We are NOT gladiators fighting each other and the lions for the entertainment of our elected officials, the lobbyists and those they represent. OUR country is about EQUAL RIGhTS for ALL. Start on your block and in your city.

Now that we are allowed to talk to our neighbors, go talk to them. Have a block party. What are the problems on YOUR block? Seniors who have no rides to the doctor? Since Mothers or single Fathers, or grandparents raising children of deployed, or PTSD children and in-laws? Hoarders that bring rodents and smell to the neighborhood? Disabled, or elderly that need help cleaning up, and maintaining their property??? How can the neighborhood figure it out. We USED to have big families that helped each other. We USED to have religious and community groups that helped their own members and seniors and disabled people. Now we all sound like Ebenezer Scrooge, "are there no work houses, are their no debtor's prisons" (Dickens, A Christmas Carol).

If we want to unify, we do not have to expect to start with 320 Million people, we can start with ourselves, our family, and our own block……then move on. Inspire others to do the same.

If immigrants want what they came to America for, they need to join in.

List the addresses on YOUR block. Begin to ask, one house at a time, if the family there will be part of helping America live happily ever after...........have a block party.

We were asked to "clean up" major areas of Los Angeles and Oakland of gangs at a time when the gang problem had grown to a point where these areas where more deadly than real war zones.

Many people had ideas of what to do. We asked those who lived there to be part of the solution. When we asked the big gangsters to ask the slum landlords. to clean up their properties and control their tenants, the gangsters were surprised. We said, "if we ask them, they ignore us, if community groups come in and attempt to clean it up, it is back the same in a few weeks, litter, graffiti, big trash and old cars in the yards. If the city comes out and demands they clean it up, nothing happens at all. If YOU tell the landlords to clean it up, and the tenants to help and keep it clean, they will be out in the night to get it cleaned by the deadline.

We had asked the gangsters if they wanted their children to grow up in the same old no chance for anything life they had grown up in, the choice between being a poorly paid houseworker, or laborer, or a gangster was not a choice. We added that if THEY told the kids to do well in school, the kids WOULD be doing well in school. People were afraid, and rightly so, of those gangsters.

YOUR block may not have gangsters such as these, just foreign or out of state landlords that are going to foreclose on mortgages, or evict on expensive rents not paid due to job loss during Covid. If you whole block gets together with other blocks and "expects" the city and county and state to resolve the problems without paying the banks and slum landlords huge amounts of taxpayer money, settlements can be found, we do not know what YOUR settlement will look like. For those who are getting their jobs back, maybe just putting the entire mortgage back payments on the end, without additional interest would save people's homes, and save foreclosures, and maybe even save banks from short selling foreclosed properties.

List some problems on your block, and local schools, and city that concern you.

For each problem listed, can you find others in your block, school, and city that are also concerned? List who is responsible for each concern......the School superintendent, the city council, the police, the parents, the teachers union, your state representative, your Congressperson.......look them up and go visit them in groups, or send petitions to them and local news media to demand change.

CHAPTER FIVE

YOUR County

Many city and school problems are best addressed at the county level. Find out if the school personnel, Principal, teachers union and bus drivers will sign petitions for changes so everyone can "live happily ever after".

Make a list of those who want the changes. Ask the kids themselves. Graffiti and vandalism are huge problems and cost a lot of money that could be better spend for sports fields, local swimming pools, and modern local libraries with wi-fi so all children and teens can study there if they behave to help others study, not just disrupt and vandalize public property.

One of the big reasons people want to come to America is public schools, and a chance for a free education. Many of the children are NOT made aware of this fact, or that every penny spent on repairing vandalism or graffiti means less money for good things, such as music, art and drama classes.

List a group of people who WILL help with getting the whole community involved in stopping bullying, graffiti and vandalism to help raise money for needed community projects.

Invite the kids, especially those known to vandalize, do graffiti and be bullies.....not to punish, or humiliate them, but to get them on the top committee to get the kids ALL involved. It has worked for us always.

CHAPTER SIX

Your State

Find out who your state representatives are. go and visit the union leadership, get them to help the community be part of the schools, no longer just followers in a game that is not succeeding. If ONE child is killed in a drive by, or one senior injured or killed in a mugging by a youth, something is not working. Get those state representatives on board. Get the kids to help you get those state representatives on board.

Get a notebook, and list the problems for each block, for each city, for the schools in your city, and for your county.........be prepared, ask the teens and college students to help you prepare the proposals to send to the state officials, and elected politicians.

CHAPTER SEVEN

Your country

America is a unique experiment in human government. It is the first time someone has taken time (it was Benjamin Franklin) to go to live with the Native Nations to find out how they had huge confederacies that had protected nature, and lived in peace for centuries until the europeans came. America is a unique blend of many cultures, and something new, that as the flaws were found, has, even with civil war, and huge riots at times, and gigantic protests over *the draft and wars that many people, notably the soldiers did NOT find to be a threat to America, and wanted to end those wars against other Native Nations that saw no need to die and turn their lands and assets over to foreign greedy people just because they had troops and weapons to back them up.*

OF the PEOPLE, By the PEOPLE and for the PEOPLE, never before to most europeans was the heard of. The Constitution gave THE PEOPLE the rights, NOT those they elected.

WRITE to those elected to do what YOU the PEOPLE need to make American live happily ever after.....ALL of us.

STOP being part of the hate and division that is harming our core concepts. Whether citizens, or immigrants, or undocumented immigrants, ask every person on your block, in our city, your schools, your county, and state to join to help America live happily ever after.

Nelson Mandela was elected into a country filled with rage and anger, bitterness and no way to unite. He had a series of hearings, to tell the truth, NOT to punish, but to bring out the truth, to help everyone know the horrors, and to cleanse many of their wrongdoing, and to give other the chance to forgive, not just be told to forget.

HOW can we, Americans do the same. HOW can we listen to all, and come together to create an America that has clean air, water, and restore the raped and destroyed nature. Even the ocean is dying, yet huge corporations have begun to take part in finding new ways to support the clean up, restoration, and restore the animals and plants. To restore the family farms, and private businesses while NOT ruining the bigger businesses that employ so many and supply many products. How can we manage and resolve the problems. Surely it is not by hate and division.

CHAPTER EIGHT

Your interest in global living happily ever after.

How I got started: I joined the Jane Goodall Roots and Shoots and helped a local group create a small project to spay and neuter one million animals MORE, over five years.

Environment is ALL of our DUTY.

Getting along without war, and surely without nuclear war that will in the reality leave the entire earth dead from radiation for at least seventy years, helping all of the nations in critical times.

These are all realistic goals, IF we work together and IF we start small, and with ourselves, our families, block, city, county, nation and globally help as we can. God bless.

CHAPTER NINE

Starting Over after Covid in every way:

As noted in every chapter of this book, each one of us, on these lands, whether First Nations, Americans of every category, including immigrants, legal here, or illegal and/or undocumented immigrants NEEDS to make a commitment to learn what America is supposed to be about, and to support that vision.

CHAPTER TEN

Closing:

It is with deep prayer that all of our volunteers, students and staff pray for America to unify and establish a country that lives WITH the vision of the Founders, and the forgiveness of the First Nations for the genocide and theft of their lands and murder of all of nature that in their culture was the DUTY our Creator gave them to protect, not exploit.

God bless us everyone, of every religious background, and those who do not have or believe in the God and/or Creator many others believe in.

36

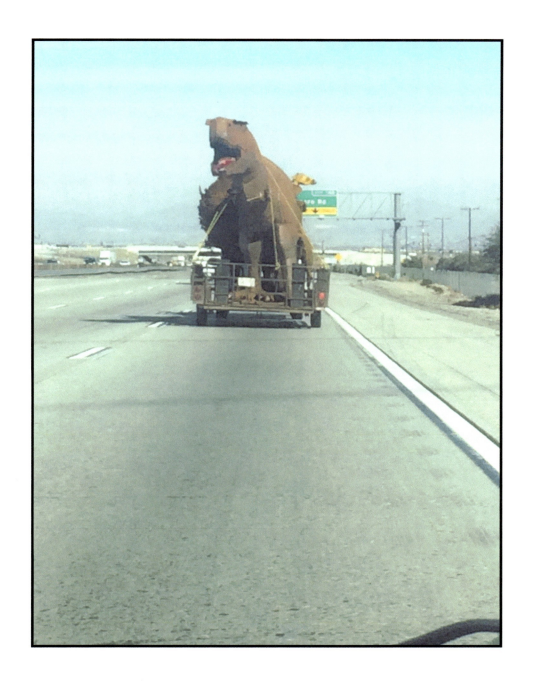

Closing;

Other books in our programs:

Closing and Other Books by Author and team

Closing:

All of our group of books, and workbooks contain some work pages, and/or suggestions for the reader, and those teaching these books to make notes, to go to computer, and libraries and ask others for information to help these projects work their best.

To utilize these to their fullest, make sure YOU model the increased thoughts and availability of more knowledge to anyone you share these books and workbooks with in classes, or community groups.

Magazines are, as noted in most of the books, a wonderful place to look for and find ongoing research and information. Online search engines often bring up new research in the areas, and newly published material.

We all have examples of how we learned and who it was that taught us.

One of the strangest lessons I have learned was walking to a shoot in downtown Los Angeles. The person who kindly told me to park my truck in Pasadena, and take the train had been unaware that the weekend busses did NOT run early in the morning when the crews had to be in to set up. That person, being just a participant, was going much later in the day, taking a taxi, and had no idea how often crews do NOT carry purses with credit cards, large amounts of cash, and have nowhere to carry those items, because the crew works hard, and fast during a set up and tear down and after the shoot are TIRED and not looking to have to find items that have been left around, or stolen.

As I walked, I had to travel through an area of Los Angeles that had become truly run down and many homeless were encamped about and sleeping on the sidewalks and in alleys. I saw a man, that having worked in an ER for many years I realized was DEAD. I used to have thoughts about people who did not notice people needing help, I thought, this poor man, this is probably the most peace he has had in a long time. I prayed for him and went off to my unwanted walk across town. As I walked, I thought about myself, was I just heartless, or was I truly thinking this was the only moment of peace this man had had for a long time and just leaving him to it. What good were upset neighbors, and police, fire trucks and ambulances going to do. He was calmly, eyes open, staring out at a world that had failed him while alive, why rush to disturb him now that nothing could be done.

I did make sure he was DEAD. He was, quite cold rigid.

I learned that day that it is best to do what a person needs, NOT what we need.

Learning is about introspection and grounding of material. Passing little tests on short term memory skills and not knowing what it all means is NOT education, or teaching.

As a high school student, in accelerated Math and Science programs, in which I received 4.0 grades consistently, I walked across a field, diagonally, and suddenly all that math and science made sense, it was not just exercises on paper I could throw answers back on paper, but I realized had NO clue as to what it all really meant.

OTHER BOOKS by this author, and team

Most, if not all, of these books are written at a fourth grade level. FIrst, the author is severely brain damaged from a high fever disease caused by a sample that came in the mail, without a warning that it had killed during test marketing. During the law suit, it was discovered that the corporation had known prior to mailing out ten million samples, WITHOUT warnings of disease and known deaths, and then NOT telling anyone after a large number of deaths around the world started. Second, the target audience is high risk youth, and young veterans, most with a poor education before signing into, or being drafted into the military as a hope Many of our veterans are Vietnam or WWII era.

Maybe those recruiting promises would come true. They would be trained, educated, and given chance for a home, and to protect our country and its principles. Watch the movies Platoon, and Born on the Fourth of July as well as the Oliver Stone series on history to find out how these dreams were meet.

DO NOT bother to write and tell us of grammar or spelling errors. We often wrote these books and workbooks fast for copyrights. We had learned our lessons about giving our material away when one huge charity asked us for our material, promising a grant, Instead, we heard a couple of years later they had built their own VERY similar project, except theirs charged for services, ours were FREE, and theirs was just for a small group, ours was training veterans and others to spread the programs as fast as they could.. They got a Nobel Peace prize. We keep saying we are not bitter, we keep saying we did not do our work to get awards, or thousands of dollars of grants....but, it hurts. Especially when lied to and that group STILL sends people to US for help when they can not meet the needs, or the veterans and family can not afford their "charitable" services. One other group had the nerve to send us a Cease and Desist using our own name. We said go ahead and sue, we have proof of legal use of this name for decades. That man had the conscience to apologize, his program was not even FOR veterans or first responders, or their families, nor high risk kids. But we learned. Sometimes life is very unfair.

We got sued again later for the same issue. We settled out of Court as our programs were just restarting and one of the veterans said, let's just change that part of the name and keep on training veterans to run their own programs. Smart young man.

Book List:

DRAGON KITES and other stories:

The Grandparents Story list will add 12 new titles this year. We encourage every family to write their own historic stories. That strange old Aunt who when you listen to her stories left a rich and well regulated life in the Eastern New York coastal fashionable families to learn Telegraph messaging and go out to the old west to LIVE her life. That old Grandfather or Grandmother who was sent by family in other countries torn by war to pick up those "dollars in the streets" as noted in the book of that title.

Books in publication, or out by summer 2021

Carousel Horse: A Children's book about equine therapy and what schools MIGHT be and are in special private programs.

Carousel Horse: A smaller version of the original Carousel Horse, both contain the workbooks and the screenplays used for on site stable programs as well as lock down programs where the children and teens are not able to go out to the stables.

Spirit Horse II: This is the work book for training veterans and others interested in starting their own Equine Therapy based programs. To be used as primary education sites, or for supplementing public or private school programs. One major goal of this book is to copyright our founding material, as we gave it away freely to those who said they wanted to help us get grants. They did not. Instead they built their own programs, with grant money, and with donations in small, beautiful stables and won....a Nobel Peace Prize for programs we invented. We learned our lessons, although we do not do our work for awards, or grants, we DO not like to be ripped off, so now we copyright.

Reassessing and Restructuring Public Agencies; This book is an over view of our government systems and how they were expected to be utilized for public betterment. This is a Fourth Grade level condemnation of a PhD dissertation that was not accepted be because the mentor thought it was "against government" .. The first paragraph noted that a request had been made, and referrals given by the then White House.

Reassessing and Restructuring Public Agencies; TWO. This book is a suggestive and creative work to give THE PEOPLE the idea of taking back their government and making the money spent and the agencies running SERVE the PEOPLE ;not politicians. This is NOT against government, it is about the DUTY of the PEOPLE to oversee and control government before it overcomes us.

Could This Be Magic? A Very Short Book. This is a very short book of pictures and the author's personal experiences as the Hall of Fame band VAN HALEN practiced in her garage. The pictures are taken by the author, and her then five year old son. People wanted copies of the pictures, and permission was given to publish them to raise money for treatment and long term Veteran homes.

Carousel TWO: Equine therapy for Veterans. publication pending 2021

Carousel THREE: Still Spinning: Special Equine therapy for women veterans and single mothers. This book includes TWELVE STEPS BACK FROM BETRAYAL for soldiers who have been sexually assaulted in the active duty military and help from each other to heal, no matter how horrible the situation. publication pending 2021

LEGAL ETHICS: AN OXYMORON. A book to give to lawyers and judges you feel have not gotten the justice of American Constitution based law (Politicians are great persons to gift with this book). Publication late 2021

PARENTS CAN LIVE and raise great kids.

Included in this book are excerpts from our workbooks from KIDS ANONYMOUS and KIDS JR, and A PARENTS PLAIN RAP (to teach sexuality and relationships to their children. This program came from a copyrighted project thirty years ago, which has been networked into our other programs. This is our training work book. We asked AA what we had to do to become a real Twelve Step program as this is considered a quasi twelve step program children and teens can use to heal BEFORE becoming involved in drugs, sexual addiction, sexual trafficking and relationship woes, as well as unwanted, neglected and abused or having children murdered by parents not able to deal with the reality of parenting. Many of our original students were children of abuse and neglect, no matter how wealthy. Often the neglect was by society itself when children lost parents to illness, accidents or addiction. We were told, send us a copy and make sure you call it quasi. The Teens in the first programs when surveyed for the outcome research reports said, WE NEEDED THIS EARLIER. SO they helped younger children invent KIDS JR. Will be republished in 2021 as a documentary of the work and success of these projects.

Addicted To Dick. This is a quasi Twelve Step program for women in domestic violence programs mandated by Courts due to repeated incidents and danger, or actual injury or death of their children.

Addicted to Dick 2018 This book is a specially requested workbook for women in custody, or out on probation for abuse to their children, either by themselves or their sexual partners or spouses. The estimated national number for children at risk at the time of request was three million across the nation. During Covid it is estimated that number has risen. Homelessness and undocumented families that are unlikely to be reported or found are creating discussion of a much larger number of children maimed or killed in these domestic violence crimes. THE most important point in this book is to force every local school district to train teachers, and all staff to recognize children at risk, and to report their family for HELP, not punishment. The second most important part is to teach every child on American soil to know to ask for help, no matter that parents, or other relatives or known adults, or unknown adults have threatened to kill them for "telling". Most, if not all paramedics, emergency rooms, and police and fire stations are trained to protect the children and teens, and get help for the family.. PUNISHMENT is not the goal, eliminating childhood abuse and injury or death at the hands of family is the goal of all these projects. In some areas JUDGES of child and family courts were taking training and teaching programs themselves to HELP. FREE..

Addicted to Locker Room BS. This book is about MEN who are addicted to the lies told in locker rooms and bars. During volunteer work at just one of several huge juvenile lock downs, where juveniles who have been convicted as adults, but are waiting for their 18th birthday to be sent to adult prisons, we noticed that the young boys and teens had "big" ideas of themselves, learned in locker rooms and back alleys. Hundreds of these young boys would march, monotonously around the enclosures, their lives over. often facing long term adult prison sentences.

The girls, we noticed that the girls, for the most part were smart, had done well in school, then "something" happened. During the years involved in this volunteer work I saw only ONE young girl who was so mentally ill I felt she was not reachable, and should be in a locked down mental health facility for help; if at all possible, and if teachers, and others had been properly trained, helped BEFORE she gotten to that place, lost in the horror and broken of her childhood and early teen years.

We noticed that many of the young women in non military sexual assault healing programs were "betrayed" in many ways, by step fathers, boyfriends, even fathers, and mothers by either molestation by family members, or allowing family members or friends of parents to molest these young women, often as small children. We asked military sexually assaulted young women to begin to volunteer to help in the programs to heal the young girls and teens, it helped heal them all.

There was NOTHING for the boys that even began to reach them until our research began on the locker room BS theory of life destruction and possible salvaging by the boys themselves, and men in prisons who helped put together something they thought they MIGHT have heard before they ended up in prison.

Americans CAN Live Happily Ever After. Parents edition.One

Americans CAN Live Happily Ever After. Children's edition Two.

Americans CAN Live Happily Ever After. Three. After Covid. This book includes "Welcome to America" a requested consult workbook for children and youth finding themselves in cages, auditoriums on cots, or in foster group homes or foster care of relatives or non-relatives with NO guidelines for their particular issues. WE ASKED the kids, and they helped us write this fourth grade level workbook portion of this book to help one another and each other. Written in a hurry! We were asked to use our expertise in other youth programs, and our years of experience teaching and working in high risk youth programs to find something to help.

REZ CHEESE Written by a Native American /WASP mix woman. Using food, and thoughts on not getting THE DIABETES, stories are included of a childhood between two worlds.

REZ CHEESE TWO A continuation of the stress on THE DIABETES needing treatment and health care from birth as well as recipes, and stories from Native America, including thoughts on asking youth to help stop the overwhelming numbers of suicide by our people.

BIG LIZ: LEADER OF THE GANG Stories of unique Racial Tension and Gang Abatement projects created when gangs and racial problems began to make schools unsafe for our children.

DOLLARS IN THE STREETS, ghost edited for author Lydia Caceras, the first woman horse trainer at Belmont Park.

95 YEARS of TEACHING:

A book on teaching, as opposed to kid flipping

Two teachers who have created and implemented systems for private and public education a combined 95 plus years of teaching talk about experiences and realities and how parents can get involved in education for their children. Included are excerpts from our KIDS ANONYMOUS and KIDS JR workbooks of over 30 years of free youth programs.

A HORSE IS NOT A BICYCLE. A book about pet ownership and how to prepare your children for responsible pet ownership and along the way to be responsible parents. NO ONE needs to own a pet, or have a child, but if they make that choice, the animal, or child deserves a solid, caring forever home.

OLD MAN THINGS and MARE'S TALES. this is a fun book about old horse trainers I met along the way. My husband used to call the old man stories "old man things", which are those enchanting and often very effective methods of horse, pet, and even child rearing. I always said I brought up my children and my students the same as I had trained horses and dogs......I meant that horses and dogs had taught me a lot of sensible, humane ways to bring up an individual, caring, and dream realizing adult who was HAPPY and loved.

STOP TALKING, DO IT

ALL of us have dreams, intentions, make promises. This book is a workbook from one of our programs to help a person make their dreams come true, to build their intentions into goals, and realities, and to keep their promises. One story from this book, that inspired the concept is a high school kid, now in his sixties, that was in a special ed program for drug abuse and not doing well in school. When asked, he said his problem was that his parents would not allow him to buy a motorcycle. He admitted that he did not have money to buy one, insure one, take proper driver's education and licensing examinations to own one, even though he had a job. He was asked to figure out how much money he was spending on drugs. Wasting his own money, stealing from his parents and other relatives, and then to figure out, if he saved his own money, did some side jobs for neighbors and family until he was 18, he COULD afford the motorcycle and all it required to legally own one. In fact, he did all, but decided to spend the money on college instead of the motorcycle when he graduated from high school. His priorities had changed as he learned about responsible motorcycle ownership and risk doing the assignments needed for his special ed program. He also gave up drugs, since his stated reason was he could not have a motorcycle, and that was no longer true, he COULD have a motorcycle, just had to buy it himself, not just expect his parents to give it to him.

Printed in the United States
by Baker & Taylor Publisher Services